Hanuman Chalisa

Published in Sanskriti Press
by Rupa Publications India Pvt. Ltd 2025
161-B/4, Gulmohar House,
Yusuf Sarai Community Centre,
New Delhi 110049

Sales centres:
Bengaluru Chennai
Hyderabad Kolkata Mumbai

Edition copyright © Rupa Publications India Pvt. Ltd 2025

All rights reserved.
No part of this publication may be reproduced, transmitted,
or stored in a retrieval system, in any form or by any means, electronic,
mechanical, photocopying, recording or otherwise, without the prior
permission of the publisher.

P-ISBN: 978-93-6156-167-2
E-ISBN: 978-93-6156-087-3

Third impression 2025

10 9 8 7 6 5 4 3

Printed in India

This book is sold subject to the condition that it shall not, by way of
trade or otherwise, be lent, resold, hired out, or otherwise circulated,
without the publisher's prior consent, in any form of binding or cover
other than that in which it is published.

Introduction

The Hanuman Chalisa is a highly revered devotional hymn dedicated to Lord Hanuman, one of the most prominent figures in Hindu mythology. It was written by the poet-saint Tulsidas in the 16th century and is considered one of the most widely recited prayers in Hinduism. The Chalisa consists of forty verses (the term 'Chalisa' meaning forty), and it praises Lord Hanuman's strength, devotion, wisdom, and courage.

Tulsidas, known for his deep devotion to Lord Ram, composed the Hanuman Chalisa in Awadhi, a dialect of Hindi. The hymn serves as both an offering of praise to Hanuman and a prayer seeking his blessings for protection, strength, and spiritual well-being. It begins with two introductory Dohas (couplets) and is followed by forty Chaupais (quatrains), each detailing the qualities, feats, and virtues of Hanuman.

The significance of the Hanuman Chalisa lies in its ability to invoke Lord Hanuman's divine blessings. Hanuman is revered not only for his immense physical strength but also for his boundless devotion to Lord Ram, and his wisdom and courage. The Chalisa recounts various stories from the *Ramayana*, highlighting Hanuman's role in helping Lord Ram rescue Sita from the demon king Ravana. Through these stories, the hymn emphasizes Hanuman's qualities as the ultimate devotee—humble, courageous, and selfless.

Reciting the Hanuman Chalisa is believed to have numerous benefits. It is said to provide strength and courage to face life's challenges, remove obstacles, and bring protection from negative forces. It also promotes spiritual growth, mental peace, and physical healing. Devotees believe that by reciting it with sincerity, they can invoke Lord Hanuman's divine presence in their lives, seeking his intervention in times of difficulty or danger. It is also said to bring about relief from stress, illness, and even bad luck.

The Chalisa's power is not only spiritual but also emotional. Its verses speak to the resilience and faith that Hanuman embodies, offering guidance and comfort to those facing trials or uncertainties. Reciting the Hanuman Chalisa regularly is thought to bring solace, strengthen one's resolve, and foster a sense of divine protection.

Though the Hanuman Chalisa is often recited in its entirety, it can also be used in parts depending on the devotee's needs or time constraints. It is a common practice to recite the hymn in the morning or evening as part of a devotional routine. Some devotees also choose to chant it a specific number of times, such as 108, for spiritual reasons. The belief that Lord Hanuman removes obstacles and provides protection from evil forces makes it a popular prayer for personal and family welfare.

In conclusion, the Hanuman Chalisa is more than just a devotional song — it is a source of spiritual and emotional strength for countless devotees worldwide. Through its verses, it not only honors Lord Hanuman but also serves as a reminder of the power of faith, devotion, and perseverance. Whether for protection, healing, or strength, chanting the Hanuman Chalisa is a powerful spiritual tool that continues to inspire and uplift those who turn to it.

श्रीगुरु चरन सरोज रज, निज मनु मुकुरु सुधारि।
बरनऊं रघुबर बिमल जसु, जो दायकु फल चारि।।

Shree Guru Charan Saroj Raj,
Nij Manu Mukur Sudhaari.
Barnoo Raghuvar Bimal Jasu,
Jo Daayaku Phal Chari.

With the dust of the Guru's lotus feet, I cleanse the mirror of my mind. I describe the pure glory of Lord Ram, which grants the four fruits of life (Dharma, Artha, Kama, Moksha).

बुद्धिहीन तनु जानिके, सुमिरौं पवन-कुमार।
बल बुद्धि बिद्या देहु मोहिं, हरहु कलेस बिकार।।

Buddhiheen Tanu Jaanike,
Sumiron Pavan Kumar.
Bal Buddhi Vidya Dehu Mohi,
Harahu Kalesh Vikar.

Knowing myself to be devoid of intelligence,
I remember Pavan Kumar (Hanuman).
Grant me strength, wisdom, and knowledge,
and remove my suffering and impurities.

1

जय हनुमान ज्ञान गुन सागर ।
जय कपीस तिहुँ लोक उजागर ॥

Jai Hanuman Gyaan Gun Saagar,
Jai Kapis Tihun Lok Ujaagar.

Hail Hanuman, the ocean of wisdom and virtues. Hail the lord of monkeys, who illuminates the three worlds.

2

राम दूत अतुलित बल धामा ।
अंजनि पुत्र पवनसुत नामा ।।

Ram Doot Atulit Bal Dhaama,
Anjani Putra Pavan Sut Naama.

You are the messenger of Lord Ram and the repository of immeasurable strength. You are the son of Anjani and the wind-god, named Pavanputra.

3

महाबीर बिक्रम बजरंगी ।
कुमति निवार सुमति के संगी ॥

Mahabeer Bikram Bajrangi,
Kumati Nivaar Sumati Ke Sanghi.

You are the mighty hero, the valiant one, with a body like a thunderbolt. You dispel evil thoughts and are the companion of good intellect.

4

कंचन बरन बिराज सुबेसा ।
कानन कुंडल कुँचित केसा ॥

Kanchan Baran Biraj Subesa,
Kanan Kundal Kuncht Kesa.

Your complexion is golden, and you wear beautiful clothes. You adorn yourself with earrings and your hair is curly.

5

हाथ बज्र अरु ध्वजा बिराजे ।
काँधे मूँज जनेऊ साजे ॥

Haath Bajra Aru Dhwaja Biraje,
Kaandhe Moonj Janeu Saaje.

In your hand, you carry a mace and a flag. You wear a sacred thread made of munj grass over your shoulder.

6

शंकर सुवन केसरी नंदन ।
तेज प्रताप महा जगवंदन ॥

Shankar Suvan Kesari Nandan,
Tej Pratap Maha Jagvandan.

You are the son of Lord Shankar (Shiva) and Kesari. Your brilliance and glory are praised by the entire world.

7

विद्यावान गुनी अति चातुर ।
राम काज करिबे को आतुर ॥

Vidyaawan Guni Ati Chatur,
Ram Kaaj Karibe Ko Aatur.

You are a scholar, virtuous, and extremely clever. You are always eager to do the work of Lord Ram.

8

प्रभु चरित्र सुनिबे को रसिया ।
राम लखन सीता मनबसिया ।।

Prabhu Charitr Sunibe Ko Rasiya,
Ram Lakhun Seeta Man Basia.

You delight in listening to the stories of Lord Ram. Ram, Lakshman, and Sita reside in your heart.

9

सूक्ष्म रूप धरि सियहि दिखावा ।
विकट रूप धरि लंका जरावा ॥

Sookshm Roop Dhari Siyahi Dikhawa,
Vikat Roop Dhari Lanka Jaraawa.

You assumed a tiny form to show yourself to Sita. You assumed a terrifying form to burn down Lanka.

10

भीम रूप धरि असुर सँहारे ।
रामचंद्र के काज सवाँरे ॥

Bheem Roop Dhari Asur Sanhaare,
Ramchandra Ke Kaaj Savaare.

You assumed a huge form and destroyed the demons. You completed the tasks of Lord Ram.

11

लाय सजीवन लखन जियाए ।
श्री रघुबीर हरषि उर लाए ॥

Laay Sjeevan Lakhan Jiaye,
Shree Raghubir Harsh Uar Laaye.

You brought the life-restoring herb and revived Lakshman. Lord Raghubir (Ram) was filled with joy in his heart.

12

रघुपति कीन्ही बहुत बड़ाई ।
तुम मम प्रिय भरत-हि सम भाई ।।

Raghupati Keenee Bahut Badaai,
Tum Mam Priya Bharat Hi Sam Bhai.

Lord Ram praised you highly, saying, "You are as dear to me as my own brother Bharat."

13

सहस बदन तुम्हरो जस गावै ।
अस कहि श्रीपति कंठ लगावै ॥

Sahas Badan Tumhara Jasu Gaavai,
As Kahi Shreepati Kanth Lagaavai.

Thousands of mouths sing your glory. Saying this, Lord Ram embraced you with affection.

14

सनकादिक ब्रह्मादि मुनीसा ।
नारद सारद सहित अहीसा ।।

Sanakadik Brahmaadi Muneesa,
Narad Sardar Sahit Aheesa.

Sanaka and other sages, Brahma, Narad, Saraswati, and even the serpent king (Sheshnag) praise you.

15

यम कुबेर दिगपाल जहाँ ते ।
कवि कोविद कहि सके कहाँ ते ॥

Yam Kuber Digpaal Jahan Te,
Kavi Kovid Kahi Sake Kahan Te.

Yamraj, Kuber, and the guardians of the directions—none can fathom the extent of your power.

16

तुम उपकार सुग्रीवहि कीन्हा ।
राम मिलाय राज पद दीन्हा ॥

Tum Upkaar Sugreevahi Keenhaa,
Ram Milaye Raj Pad Deenhaa.

You helped Sugreev by uniting him with Ram and granting him the throne.

17

तुम्हरो मंत्र बिभीषण माना ।
लंकेश्वर भये सब जग जाना ।।

Tumhara Mantra Vibhishan Maana,
Lankeshwar Bhaye Sab Jag Jaana.

Vibhishan accepted your mantra, and everyone came to know that he became the ruler of Lanka.

18

जुग सहस्त्र जोजन पर भानू ।
लिल्यो ताहि मधुर फल जानू ॥

Jug Sahastra Yojan Par Bhaanu,
Lilyo Taahi Madhur Phal Jaanu.

You crossed the vast ocean, which is thousands of Yojanas wide, in a moment and brought back the sweet fruit (herb).

19

प्रभु मुद्रिका मेलि मुख माही ।
जलधि लाँघि गए अचरज नाही ॥

Prabhu Mudrika Meli Mukh Maahi,
Jaladhi Langhi Gaye Achraj Nahi.

With Lord Ram's ring in your mouth, you crossed the ocean without any difficulty.

20

दुर्गम काज जगत के जेते ।
सुगम अनुग्रह तुम्हरे तेते ॥

Durgam Kaaj Jagat Ke Jete,
Sugam Anugrah Tumhare Tete.

All the difficult tasks in the world become easy with your grace.

21

राम दुआरे तुम रखवारे ।
होत ना आज्ञा बिनु पैसारे ॥

Ram Dwaare Tum Rakhware,
Hot Na Aajna Binu Paisaare.

You are the guardian at the door of Lord Ram, and no one can enter without your permission.

22

सब सुख लहैं तुम्हारी सरना ।
तुम रक्षक काहु को डर ना ॥

Sab Sukh Lehi Tumhari Sarna,
Tum Rakshak Kahu Ko Dar Na.

All joys are found in your refuge, and with you as our protector, there is no fear.

23

आपन तेज सम्हारो आपै ।
तीनों लोक हाँक तै कापै ।।

Aapan Tej Samharo Aapai,
Teenon Lok Haank Tai Kaapai.

You keep your power under control, and by your mere roar, all three worlds tremble.

24

भूत पिशाच निकट नहि आवै ।
महावीर जब नाम सुनावै ॥

Bhoot Pishaach Nikat Nahi Aave,
Mahaveer Jab Naam Sunave.

No ghost or demon can approach when the mighty name of Hanuman is uttered.

25

नासै रोग हरे सब पीरा ।
जपत निरंतर हनुमत बीरा ॥

Naasai Rog Hare Sab Peera,
Japat Nirantar Hanumat Beera.

All diseases and pains are eradicated by constantly chanting the name of Hanuman.

26

संकट तै हनुमान छुडावै ।
मन क्रम वचन ध्यान जो लावै ॥

Sankat Tai Hanuman Chudave,
Man Kram Vachan Dhyaan Jo Laave.

Hanuman saves those who call upon him in their mind, speech, or action from all difficulties.

27

सब पर राम तपस्वी राजा ।
तिनके काज सकल तुम साजा ॥

Sab Par Ram Tapasvi Raja,
Tinke Kaaj Sakal Tum Saja.

You take care of all the work of Ram, the king of all ascetics.

28

और मनोरथ जो कोई लावै ।
सोई अमित जीवन फल पावै ।।

Aur Manorath Jo Koi Laave,
Soi Amit Jeevan Phal Paave.

Anyone who brings their desires to you will be granted the fruit of endless life.

29

चारों जुग परताप तुम्हारा ।
है परसिद्ध जगत उजियारा ॥

Chaaron Jug Prataap Tumhara,
Hai Parasiddh Jagat Ujiyaara.

Your glory shines throughout the four ages,
and the world is illuminated by your fame.

30

साधु संत के तुम रखवारे ।
असुर निकंदन राम दुलारे ॥

Saadhu Sant Ke Tum Rakhwaare,
Asur Nikandan Ram Dulare.

You are the protector of saints and sages and the destroyer of demons. Ram's dear one.

31

अष्ट सिद्धि नौ निधि के दाता ।
अस वर दीन जानकी माता ॥

Asht Siddhi Nau Nidhi Ke Daata,
As Var Deen Janaki Maata.

You are the giver of the eight siddhis (spiritual powers) and nine treasures, as blessed by Janaki (Sita).

32

राम रसायन तुम्हरे पासा ।
सदा रहो रघुपति के दासा ॥

Ram Rasayan Tumhare Paasa,
Sada Raho Raghupati Ke Daasa.

You hold the essence of Ram's nectar, and you are forever the servant of Raghupati (Lord Ram).

33

तुम्हरे भजन राम को पावै ।
जनम जनम के दुख बिसरावै ॥

Tumhare Bhajan Ram Ko Paave,
Janam Janam Ke Dukh Bisraave.

Through devotion to you, one gains the love of Ram and forgets the sorrows of many lifetimes.

34

अंतकाल रघुवरपुर जाई ।
जहाँ जन्म हरिभक्त कहाई ॥

Antkaal Raghurvarpur Jaai,
Jahan Janm Haribhakt Kahaai.

At the end of one's life, they reach the abode of Lord Ram and are recognized as a devotee of Hari.

35

और देवता चित्त ना धरई ।
हनुमत सेई सर्व सुख करई ॥

Aur Devta Chit Na Dharai,
Hanumat Seii Sarv Sukh Karai.

One should not worship other deities, for Hanuman brings all joy and happiness.

36

संकट कटै मिटै सब पीरा ।
जो सुमिरै हनुमत बलबीरा ।।

Sankat Katai Mitae Sab Peera,
Jo Sumire Hanumat Balbira.

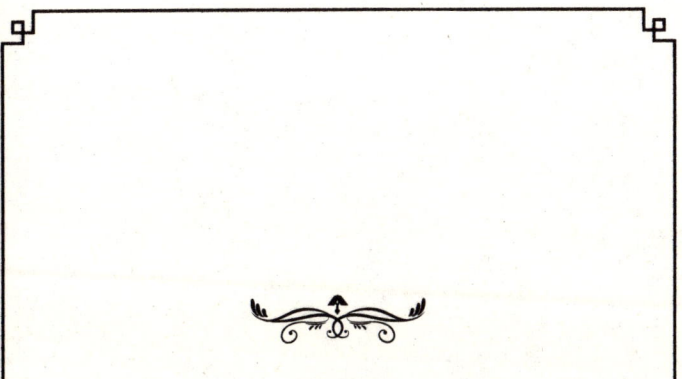

All obstacles and sufferings are destroyed by remembering the mighty Hanuman.

37

जै जै जै हनुमान गुसाईं ।
कृपा करहु गुरु देव की नाईं ॥

Jai Jai Jai Hanuman Gusaai,
Kripa Karahu Guru Dev Ki Naai.

Victory to you, O Hanuman! Bestow your grace as the Guru blesses.

38

जो सत बार पाठ कर कोई ।
छूटहिं बंदि महा सुख होई ॥

Jo Sat Baar Paath Kar Koi,
Chootahi Bandhi Maha Sukh Hoi.

Anyone who recites this *Hanuman Chalisa* 108 times will be freed from bondage and will attain supreme joy.

39

जो यह पढ़े हनुमान चालीसा ।
होय सिद्ध साखी गौरीसा ॥

Jo Yah Padhe Hanuman Chalisa,
Hoy Siddh Saakhi Gaurisa.

Whoever recites this Hanuman Chalisa will be blessed with divine success and will be a witness to Lord Shiva's glory.

40

तुलसीदास सदा हरि चेरा ।
कीजै नाथ हृदय मंह डेरा ॥

Tulsidas Sada Hari Chera,
Keeje Nath Hriday Mah Dera.

O Lord Hanuman, May I always remain a servant, a devotee to Lord Sri Ram, says Tulsidas. And, May You always reside in my heart.

पवन तनय संकट हरन, मंगल मूरति रूप ।
राम लखन सीता सहित, हृदय बसहु सुर भूप ॥

Pavan Tanay Sankat Haran,
Mangal Moorti Roop.
Ram Lakhan Seeta Sahit,
Hriday Basahu Sur Bhoop.

O son of the wind, remover of troubles, embodiment of auspiciousness, Reside in my heart along with Ram, Lakshman, and Sita, O King of Gods.

श्री हनुमान स्तुति

मनोजवं मारुत तुल्यवेगं,
जितेन्द्रियं, बुद्धिमतां वरिष्ठम् ॥

वातात्मजं वानरयुथ मुख्यं,
श्रीरामदुतं शरणम प्रपढ्ठे ॥

॥ आरती ॥

आरती कीजै हनुमान लला की ।
दुष्ट दलन रघुनाथ कला की ॥

जाके बल से गिरवर काँपे ।
रोग-दोष जाके निकट न झाँके ॥

अंजनि पुत्र महा बलदाई ।
संतन के प्रभु सदा सहाई ॥

आरती कीजै हनुमान लला की ॥

दे वीरा रघुनाथ पठाए ।
लंका जारि सिया सुधि लाये ।।

लंका सो कोट समुद्र सी खाई ।
जात पवनसुत बार न लाई ।।

आरती कीजै हनुमान लला की ।।

लंका जारि असुर संहारे ।
सियाराम जी के काज सँवारे ।।
लक्ष्मण मुर्छित पड़े सकारे ।
लाये संजिवन प्राण उबारे ।।

आरती कीजै हनुमान लला की ।।

पैठि पताल तोरि जमकारे ।
अहिरावण की भुजा उखारे ।।

बाईं भुजा असुर दल मारे ।
दाहिने भुजा संतजन तारे ।।

आरती कीजै हनुमान लला की ।।

सुर-नर-मुनि जन आरती उतरें ।
जय जय जय हनुमान उचारें ।।

कंचन थार कपूर लौ छाई ।
आरती करत अंजना माई ।।

आरती कीजै हनुमान लला की ।।

जो हनुमानजी की आरती गावे ।
बसहिं बैकुंठ परम पद पावे ।।

लंक विध्वंस किये रघुराई ।
तुलसीदास स्वामी कीर्ति गाई ।।

आरती कीजै हनुमान लला की ।
दुष्ट दलन रघुनाथ कला की ।।

।। इति संपूर्णम् ।।

||Shri Hanumant Stuti ||

Manojavam maaruta tulyavegam,
Jitendriyam, buddhimataasvarishtham ||

Vaatatmajam vanarayuth mukhyam,
Shri Ramadutam sharanam prapadye ||

|| Aarti ||

Aarti keeje Hanumaan Lala kee.
Dushta dalan Raghunath kala kee ||
Jaake bal se Girivar kaampe,
Rog-dosh jaake nikat na jhaanke ||
Anjani putra maha baldaai,
Santan ke prabhu sada sahai ||
Aarti keeje Hanumaan Lala kee ||

De veera Raghunath pathaaye,
Lanka jaari Siya sudhi laaye ||
Lanka so kot samudra see khaayi,
Jaat Pavanasut baar na laaye ||
Aarti keeje Hanumaan Lala kee ||

Lanka jaari asura sanhaare,
Siya Ram ji ke kaaj sanwaare ||

Lakshman murchhit pade sakaar,
Laaye Sanjeevan praan ubaare ||
Aarti keeje Hanumaan Lala kee ||

Paith Paatal tor Jamkaare,
Ahiravan ki bhuja ukhhaare ||
Baain bhuja asur dal maare,
Daahine bhuja santajan taare ||
Aarti keeje Hanumaan Lala kee ||

Sur-Nar-Muni jan aarti utare,
Jai Jai Jai Hanumaan uchaare ||
Kanchan thaar kaapur lau chhaayi,
Aarti karat Anjana maai ||
Aarti keeje Hanumaan Lala kee ||

Jo Hanumaanji ki aarti gaave,
Basahin Baikunth param pad paave ||
Lanka vidhwans kiye Raghurai,
Tulsidas Swami kirti gaayi ||
Aarti keeje Hanumaan Lala kee,
Dushta dalan Raghunath kala kee ||

|| Iti Sampurnam ||